Thank You God For My Scar

By Jeannette Guzman-Zarrillo

Illustrated by Aysia Valdez

Dedicated...

To all parents who have had to or are holding their child's hand through difficult times.

To the doctors, nurses and secretaries who made the hardest part of my life somewhat bearable with only their smiles, kind eyes, and hopeful words

To our family, friends, Pastor and church community: Thank you for praying for our little girl. And for the countless phone calls, encouraging texts and uplifting words. We will be forever grateful for you.

And To Layla, the strongest little girl I know.

I can do all things through Christ who strengthens me.
Philippians 4:13

All rights reserved. No part of this publication may be reproduced, distributed, or transmitted in any form or by any means, including photocopying, recording, or other electronic or mechanical methods, or by any information storage and retrieval system without the prior written permission of the publisher.

Tomorrow is a big day.

It's the first day of school, and I'm so excited! I snuggle with Sprinkles under my warm blankets and start my prayers.

Mami says that our night time prayer is a time to thank God for all of our blessings that day.

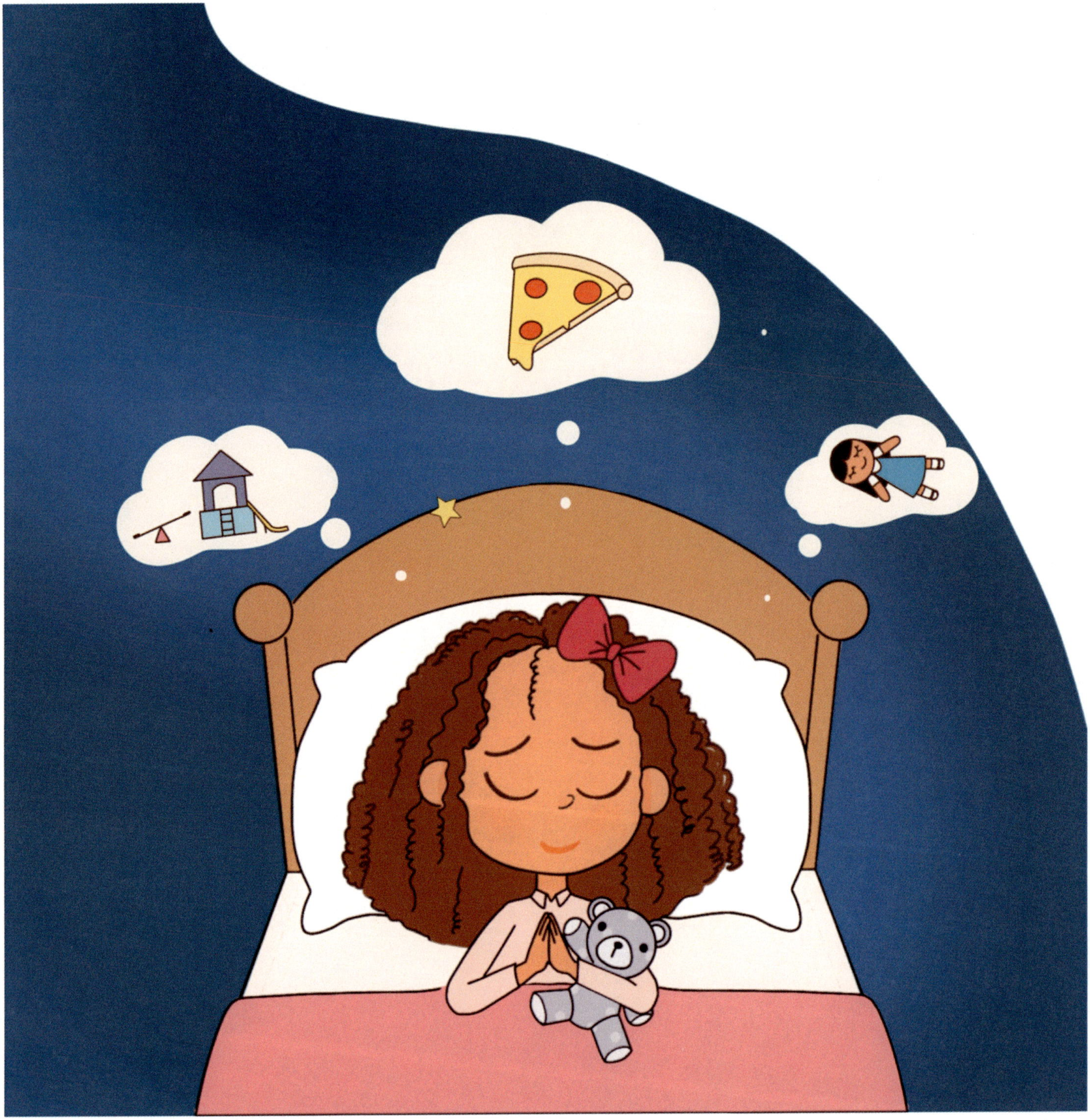

So I think about my day and all the things I want to thank God for.

"Dear God, thank you for the pizza we ate, thank you for my toys, and thank you because we went to the park today. Amen."

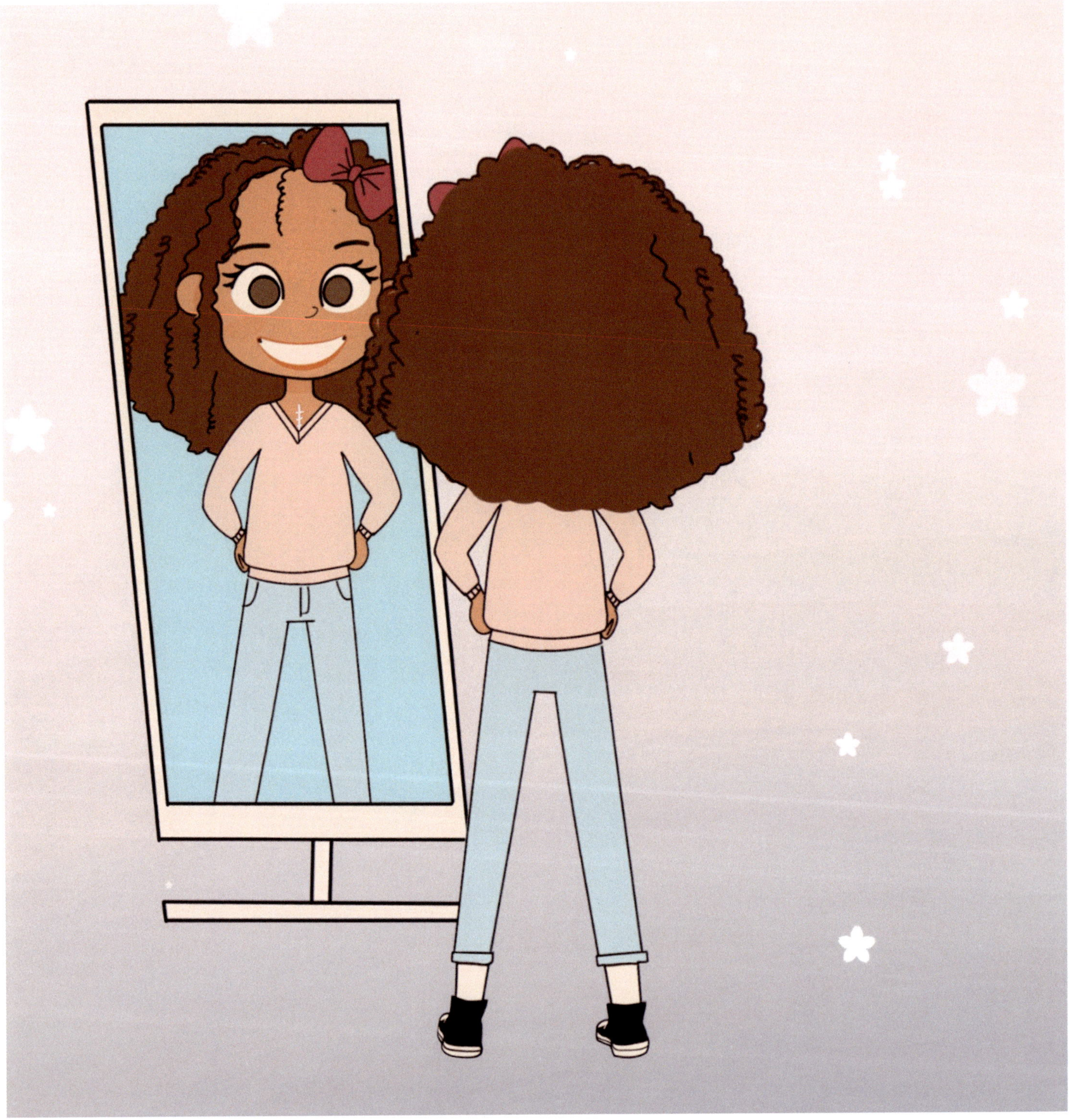

In the morning, I put on the clothes that Mami laid out for me but...

UH OH!!

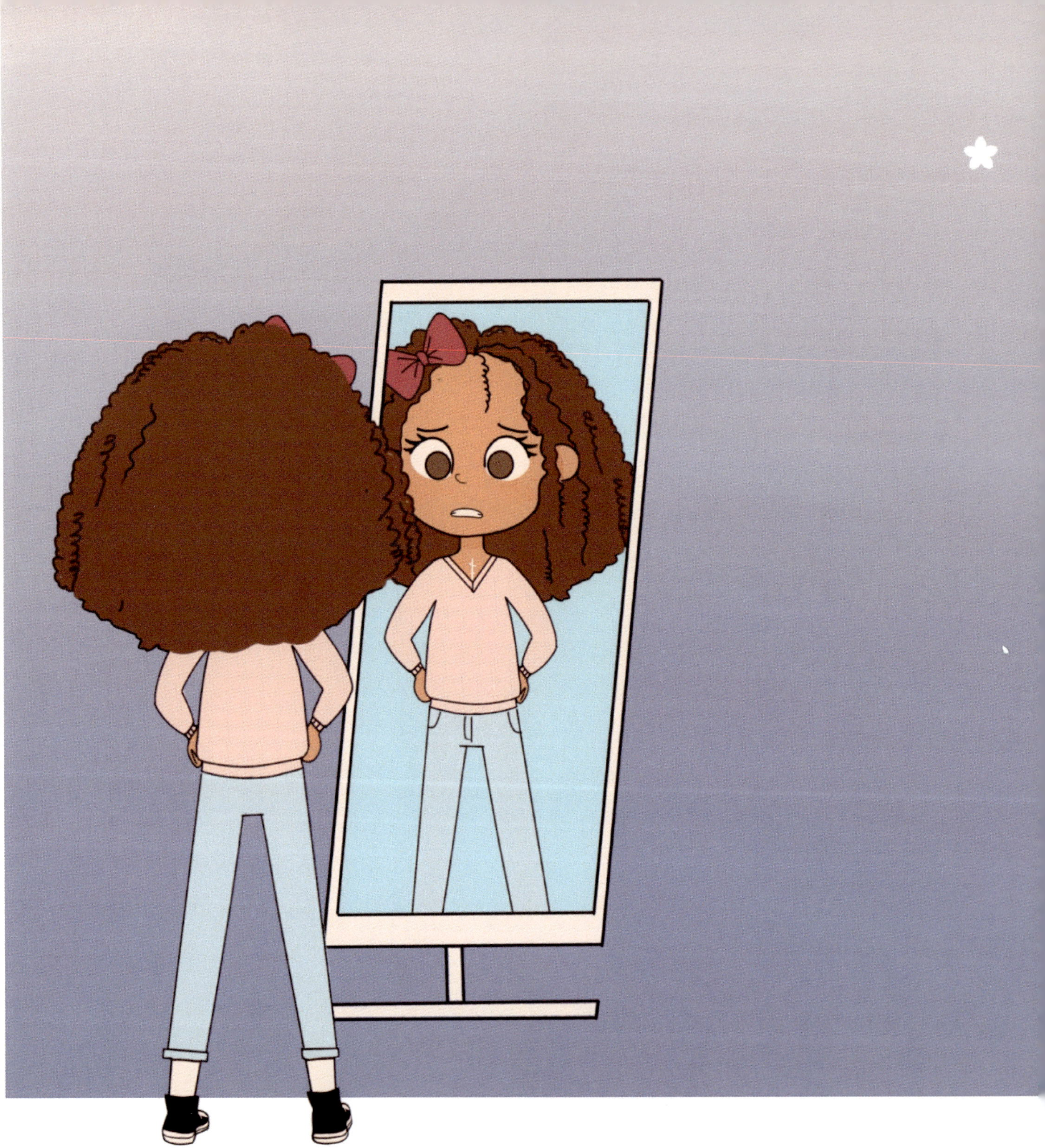

This sweater doesn't cover my scar!

"Mami!" I yell out. "I need to wear something else. My scar is showing, and I don't want anyone to see it!"

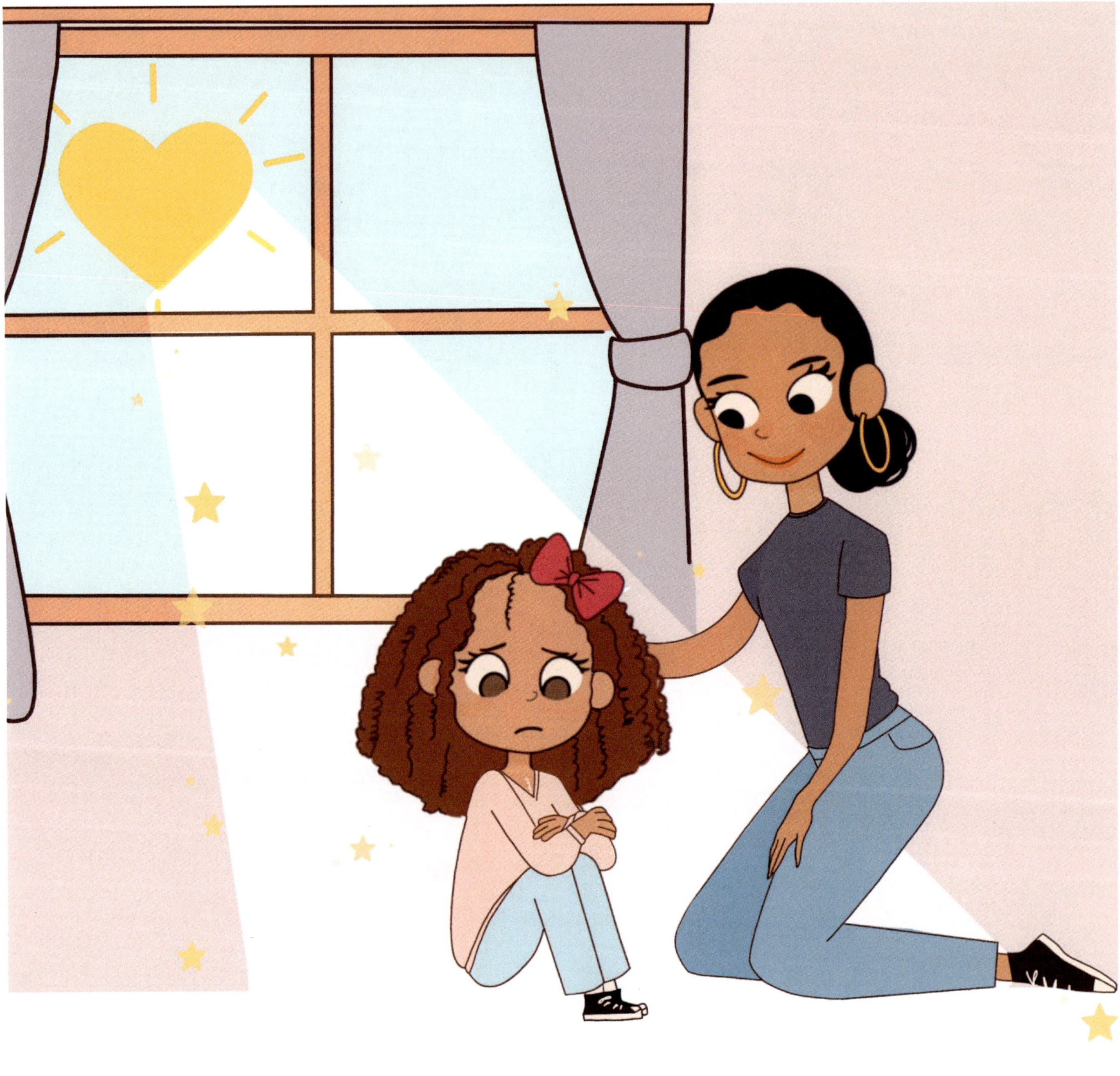

"Layla, scars are beautiful," says Mami.

"Scars mean we can go through hard things and still be ok. Your scar reminds us that you are strong and healthy. That is why no matter how my day goes, I can always thank God for your healthy heart"

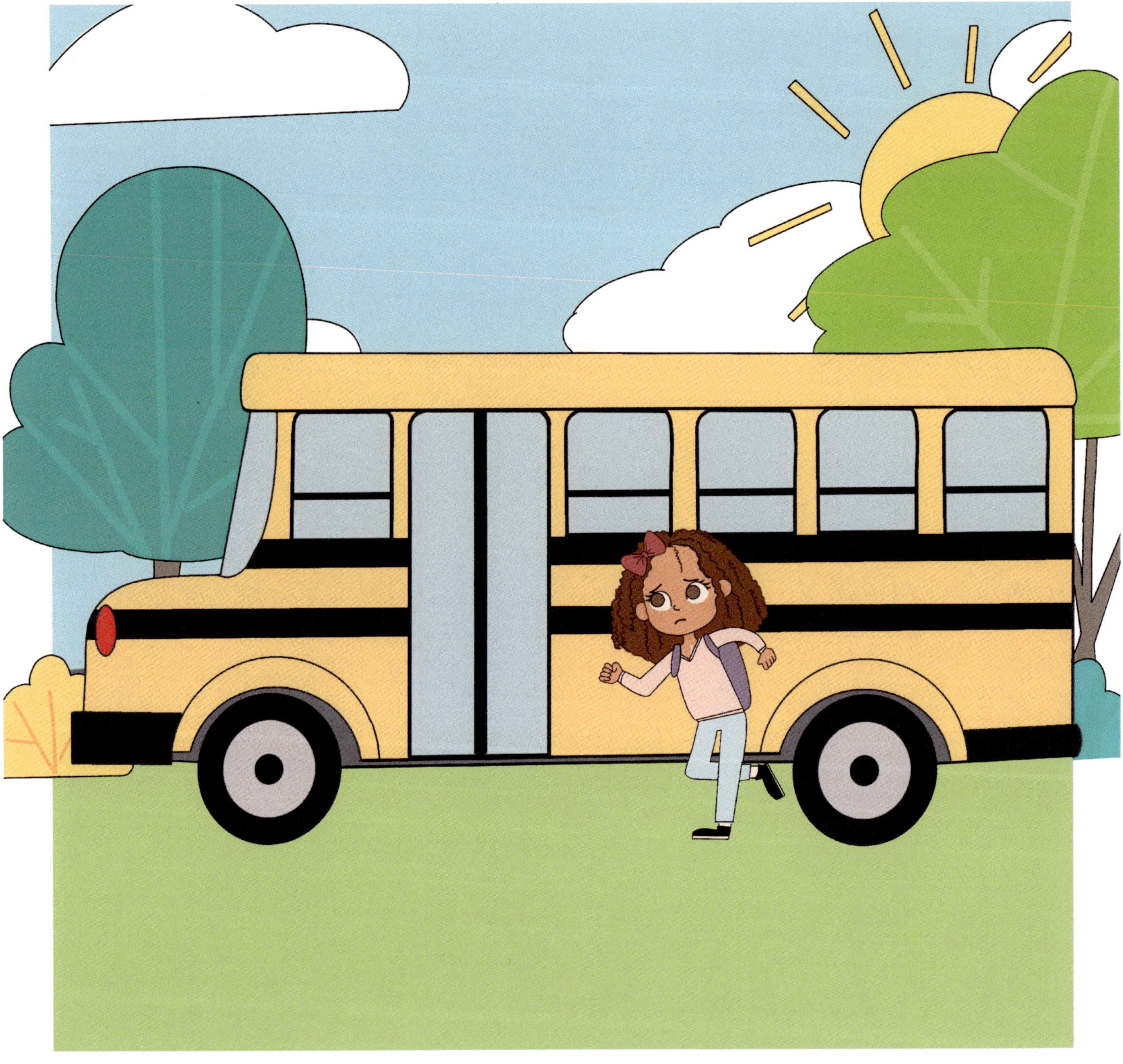

I have no time to change now -- the bus is outside!

As I'm walking toward the bus, a few thoughts pop into my head

> What are the other kids going to think when they see my scar?

> Will they make a face or say something mean?

> Will they point and stare? What will I say?

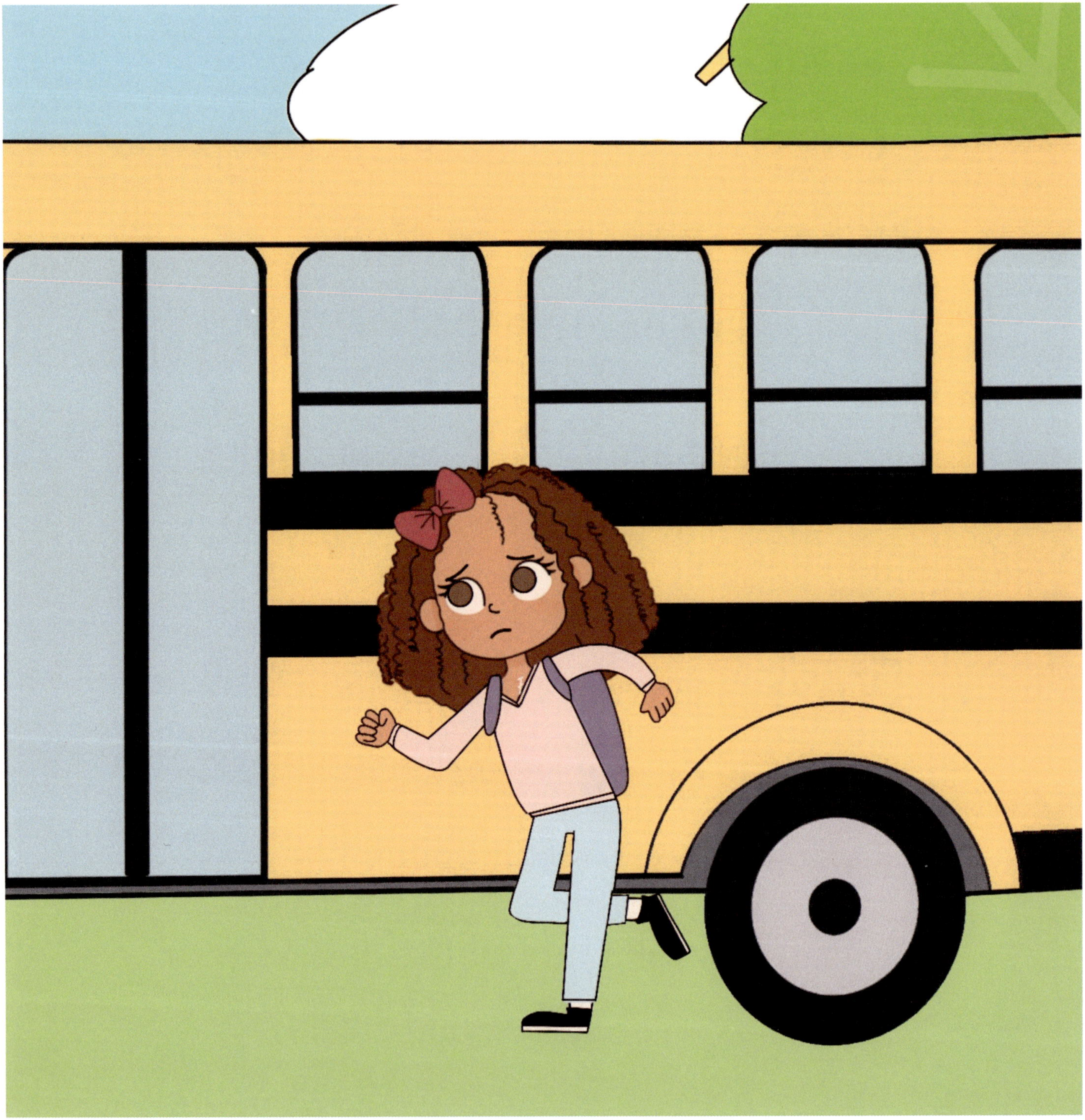

I think about running back home, but I am already on the bus. Too late to turn back now!

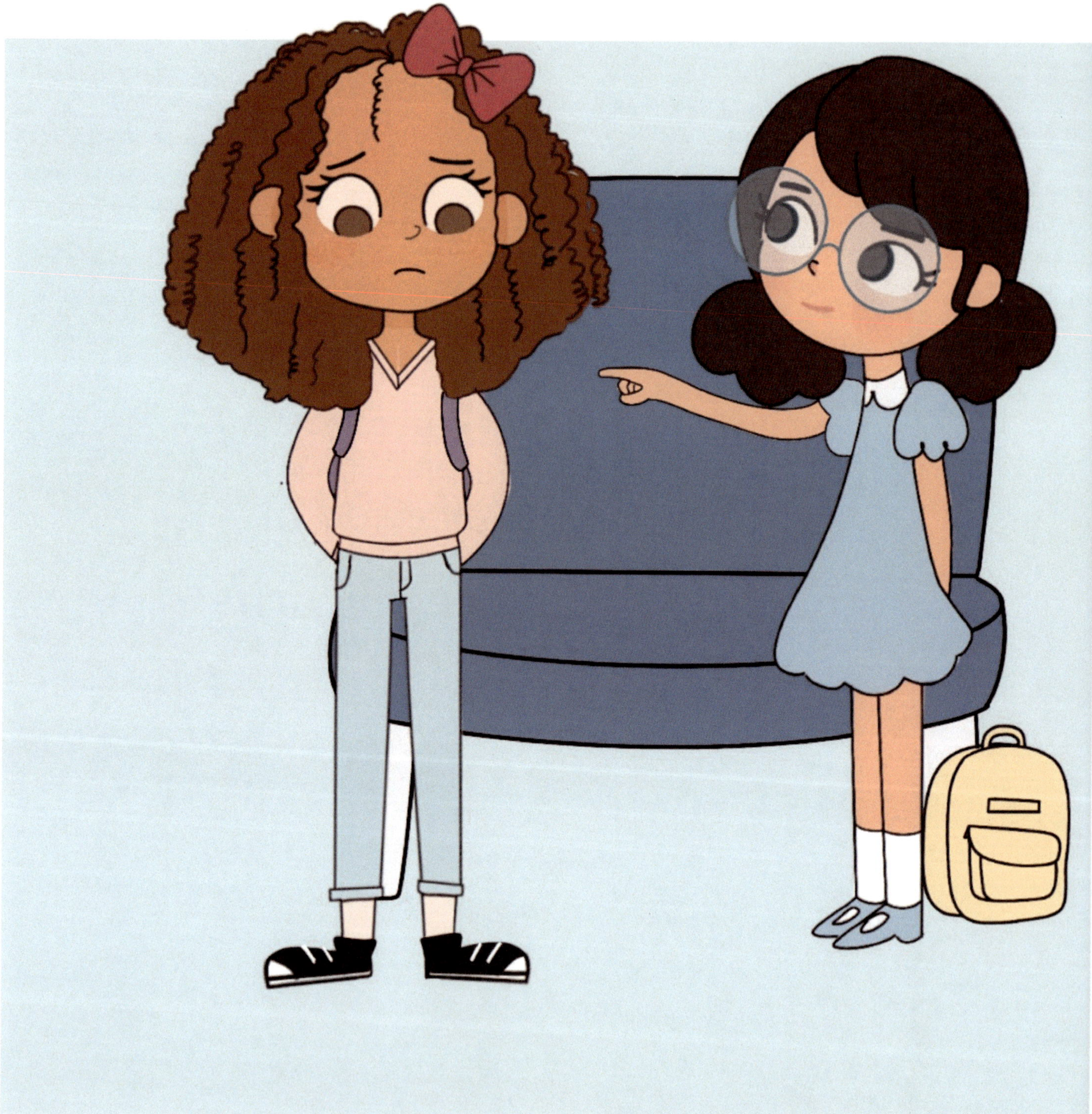

I walk to my seat with my head hung low.

Maybe if I keep it down, no one will notice me. Maybe I won't have to explain what this thing is on my chest.

"Hi, Layla!" I hear a familiar voice. It's my friend Olivia from the park. She's never seen my scar before.

Olivia starts telling me about her snacks when she stops suddenly. "Hey, what's that?" she asks.

She's pointing right at my scar!

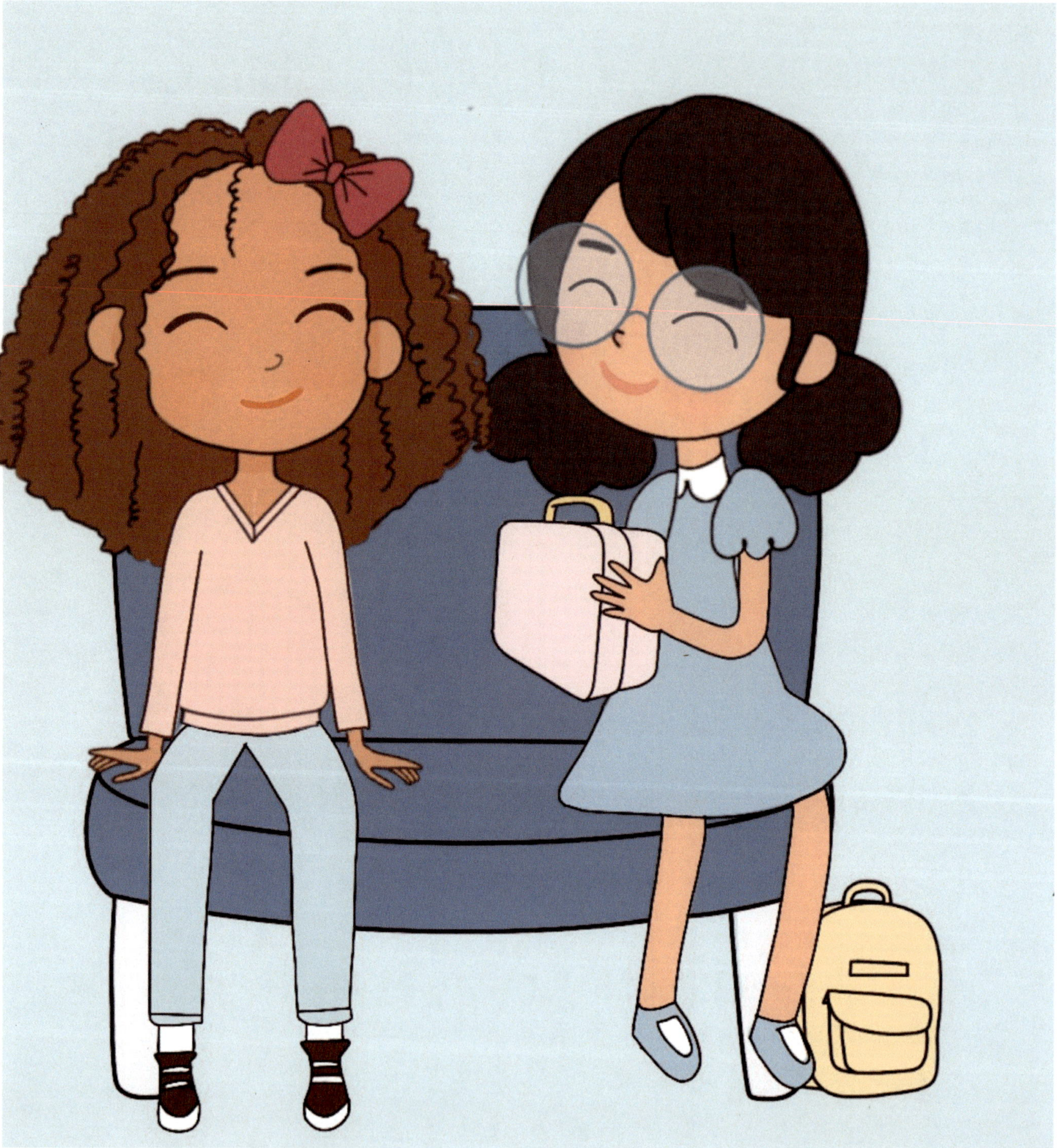

I remember Mami's words.

"Um... it's a scar... Doctors had to fix my heart when I was little... Scars mean I went through something hard and... now I'm ok, I guess...

Olivia responds, "Oh... ok.... Cool!"

"Cool?!" I never thought anyone would say "cool" about my scar!

And just like that, she goes back to showing me all the yummy snacks that her mom packed for her.

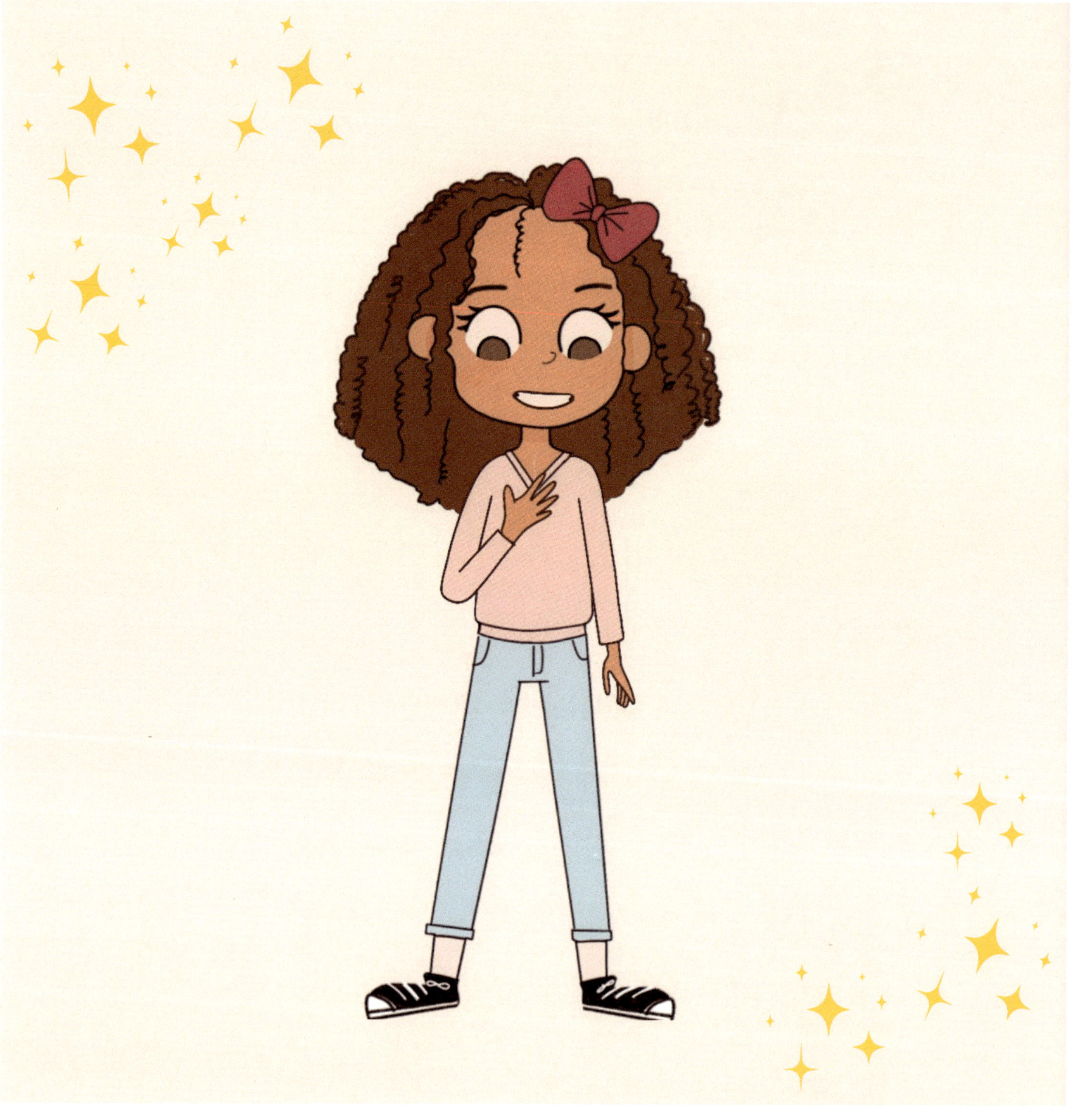

When the bus arrived at school, I was ready to walk in. This time, I was not looking down.

I felt ready to tell anyone who asked about my COOL scar!

The first half of the day is a breeze! Some kids ask about my scar, most don't. If they do, I tell them with a smile on my face and head held high:

"Yeah, this is just a cool scar I got after I had surgery to fix my heart. I was only two years old. My mom said I didn't even cry! I was asleep the whole time!"

This time, I hear different words.

"Wow!"

"Awesome!"

"Ouch!"

Before I know it, the school day is over.

When the bus stops at my house, I hop off, wave bye to my new friends, and run to my Mom.

I tell her all about my first day.

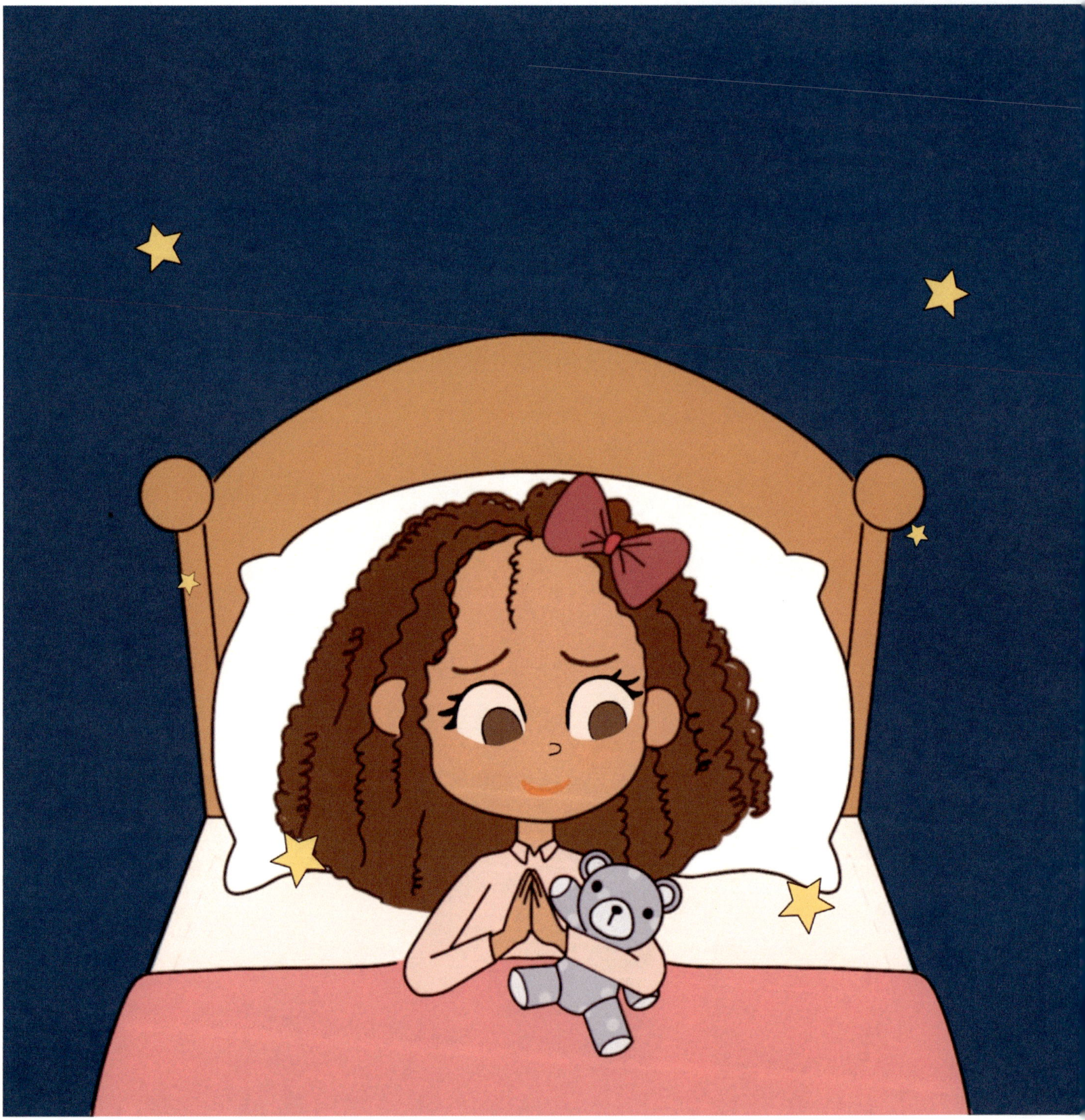

Pretty soon,
it's night-night time again.

"Come on, Sprinkles. Tomorrow is another day. It's time for bed and time to say our prayers!"

"Dear God," I start. "Thank you for today, thank you for my new friends, my nice new teacher... and thank you for my healthy heart and my COOL scar. Amen."

Made in the USA
Las Vegas, NV
25 February 2025